D1317622

# Starwatch

*Today's World in Space*

# Starwatch

J. WM. LAMBERT LIBRARY
Polk Elementary School

By David Baker

**Rourke Enterprises, Inc.**
Vero Beach, FL 32964

© 1989 Rourke Enterprises, Inc.

All rights reserved. No part of this book may be reproduced or utilized in any form or by any means, electronic or mechanical including photocopying, recording or by any information storage and retrieval system without permission in writing from the publisher.

522/B   c. 1   6/91   $12.95

**Library of Congress Cataloging-in-Publication Data**
Baker, David, 1944-
  Starwatch/by David Baker.
  p. cm. — (Today's world in space)
  Includes index.
  Summary: Describes how astronomers use telescopes and other instruments to study objects in the universe.
  ISBN 0-86592-400-7
  1. Telescope — Juvenile literature. 2. Astronautics in astronomy — Juvenile literature. [1. Telescope. 2. Astronomy.]
I. Title. II. Series: Baker, David, 1944- Today's world in space.
QB88.B35   1989                                    88-33689
522 · dc19                                            CIP
                                                     AC

# CONTENTS

# Great Telescopes

No one knows who invented the telescope, but we have a good idea who first used it to discover previously unseen things in the sky. It was Galileo, the famous professor of mathematics at the University of Padua, Italy. He made a telescope for himself in 1609 and discovered craters on the moon and moons around Jupiter. He also saw the bands of cloud in the atmosphere of Jupiter and saw markings on the planet Mars.

Until the invention of the telescope, people had various ideas about the sun, the moon, and the stars. For several thousand years they believed that the Earth was the center of the universe and that everything circled around our planet. More than 2,000 years ago, the Greeks believed the sun was the center of the universe and that the moon went around the Earth. They were right, but their ideas died out. The seventeenth century was a great time

**Stunning views of the universe are made possible only through the use of giant telescopes. This is the Omega Nebula in the constellation Sagittarius.**

The central bulge of the Andromeda galaxy, more than two million light years from Earth.

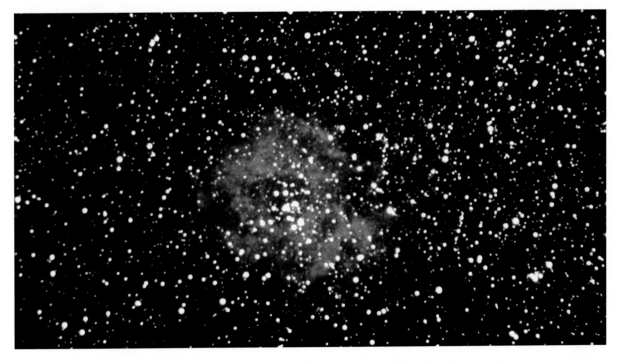

The Rosette Nebula in Monoceros takes on a magnificent splendor when seen through an optical telescope.

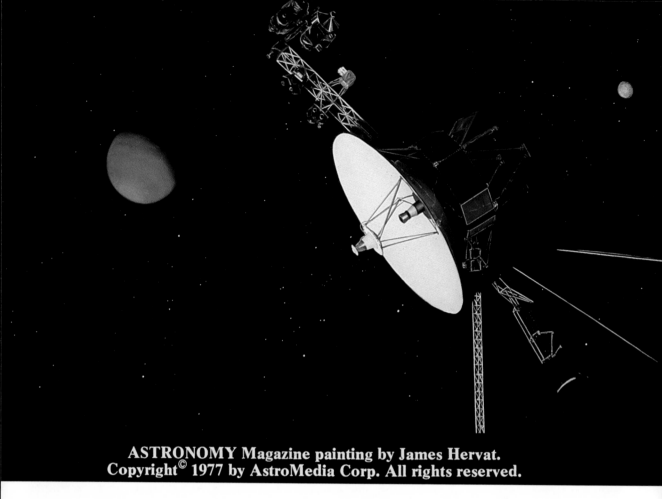

ASTRONOMY Magazine painting by James Hervat.
Copyright© 1977 by AstroMedia Corp. All rights reserved.

So far, our exploration of the universe has been limited to small probes sent to the edge of our solar system, far short of the nearest star.

for science. It was then that Galileo first used a telescope to make observations of the stars. It was also the time when Isaac Newton first correctly described the qualities of light and wrote the laws of *gravity.* Light is important because it was for thousands of years the only means by which people could discover facts about the universe. Everything we knew about the stars was understood because scientists examined the way it looked. The laws of gravity helped us understand why stars are what they are and why planets go around the sun.

The first telescopes were very small. They could be held in the hand or placed on a table. Many scientists spent hours in the dark of night with a wooden telescope, and soon the equipment was too big for a person to hold. Scientists then built observatories in

which telescopes could be enclosed and protected from the weather.

Telescopes can be divided into two main types. The most popular kind of telescope for amateurs is the *refractor,* because it is easier to handle. It is by no means an amateur's design, however, and many professional astronomers prefer to use refractors. A refractor does what all telescopes are designed to do. It gathers light and magnifies the image. A lens is contained in a long tube. As light travels through the lens, it is brought to focus down the tube and onto an eyepiece that is a magnifying lens.

The refractor was the kind of telescope used by Galileo. A typical example of a modern refractor is the 26-inch telescope at the Washington Observatory. The telescope has a lens 26 inches in diameter and has been used since 1862, the year it was completed. In 1877, the astronomer Asaph Hall used it to discover the two small moons of Mars called Phobos and Deimos. This instrument is still in use and works well.

Another refractor is the Lowell 24-inch instrument at Flagstaff, Arizona. It was installed in 1895, and Percival Lowell used it to make drawings of surface markings on the planet Mars. This refractor was used to help scientists plot moon landing sites for Apollo astronauts in the 1960s.

The other type of telescope is called the *reflector*. It was first developed by Isaac Newton at the end of the seventeenth century. It works with a combination of mirrors and lenses. The light arriving at the telescope passes down a tube and onto a mirror, where it is reflected back up the tube again. The mirror is shaped in such a way that the image converges on another mirror placed at a right-angle higher up toward the top of the tube.

**To see stars we cannot reach, astronomers use refracting or, as is the the case here, reflecting telescopes to gather more light from space.**

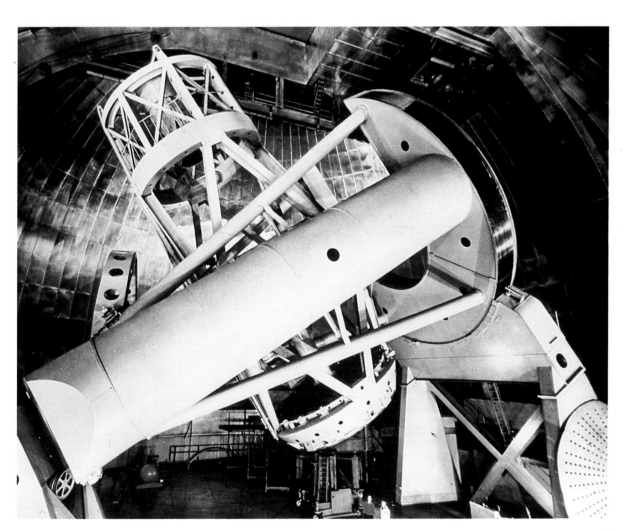

Star watching is sometimes a long, boring wait for just the right moment to view an object and hours must be spent in cramped conditions.

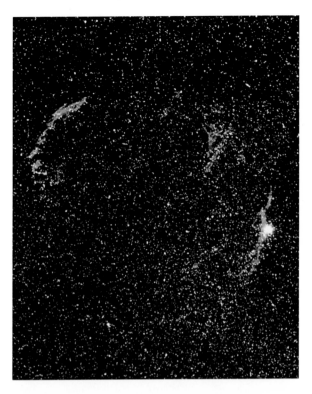

The Veil Nebula in the constellation Cygnus, showing a complete loop of gas and dust lit by millions of stars in the area.

Because it is set at a right-angle to the line of light, this mirror turns the image 90 degrees so that it comes out the side of the telescope where the eyepiece is located. The eyepiece contains the magnifying lens, which can be changed as necessary. There are several different forms of reflectors. The one just described is the Newtonian reflector, because it was designed by Isaac Newton.

Another form of reflector is called the cassegrain. In this type, light is reflected by a large mirror at the bottom of a tube, just as in the Newtonian reflector. Instead of an angled

Most observatories are located in the northern hemisphere, but this Anglo-Australian telescope allows astronomers to watch the southern sky.

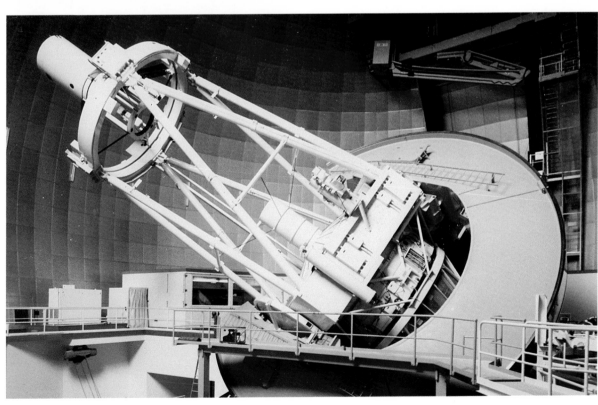

mirror, however, the light strikes another mirror that sends the reflected image back down toward the main mirror once more. A cassegrain mirror has a circular hole in the middle through which the image can now pass into the eyepiece. The eyepiece is behind the main mirror, with the hole through it, making the telescope more compact and less bulky.

The most famous reflector is the Hale reflector on Mount Palomar, California. It has a 200-inch main mirror that is 24 inches thick and weighs more than 14 tons. This telescope has been used to make some of the most important discoveries in astronomy. It was completed in 1948 and sits in a dome 135 feet high and 137 feet in diameter. The telescope is carried in a massive cage that is moved around to point at selected objects. The moving part of the telescope weighs over 500 tons.

Until the dawn of the space age the Earth-based telescope was the only way of looking at objects in the universe. Yet it gives an extremely limited view, because the atmosphere that envelops the planet causes distortion when light passes through it. The shimering effect of light on a hot day is always present for astronomers using telescopes from the surface of the Earth. At night, starlight bounces around in a telescope and sometimes makes a good view impossible.

**Large telescopes are controlled by complex electronic devices and computers to control their movement as they track the stars.**

# Astronomy from Space

There are many reasons why space-based telescopes are better than telescopes fixed to the Earth. One reason is that atmospheric distortion does not exist in space, because there is no atmosphere to play tricks with light. Another reason is that the atmosphere is getting more polluted all the time, and this has the effect of thickening up the atmosphere close to sea level. That has a very bad effect on light from stars traveling through the atmosphere to the telescope mirror or lens. One additional reason is that there are more and more artificial lights on Earth, and they throw up a background glare that distorts light from space.

Scientists have a name for such distortions. They say it is caused by atmospheric turbulence. The atmosphere can be compared to the sea, sometimes a very rough sea. Activity in towns and cities can churn up particles of dust that we cannot see with the naked eye. These particles are very fine, but they affect the way light passes through the atmosphere. This too has a bad effect on light magnified by a telescope.

If a 120-inch telescope could be placed in space, it would have 10 times the power of the 200-inch Hale reflector on Mount Palomar. It would detect stars 100 times fainter than can be seen with the Hale reflector. Because many

Earth's dense atmosphere causes distortion in the light coming from distant points of the universe and astronomers may wait many days to get pictures like this of the star Capella.

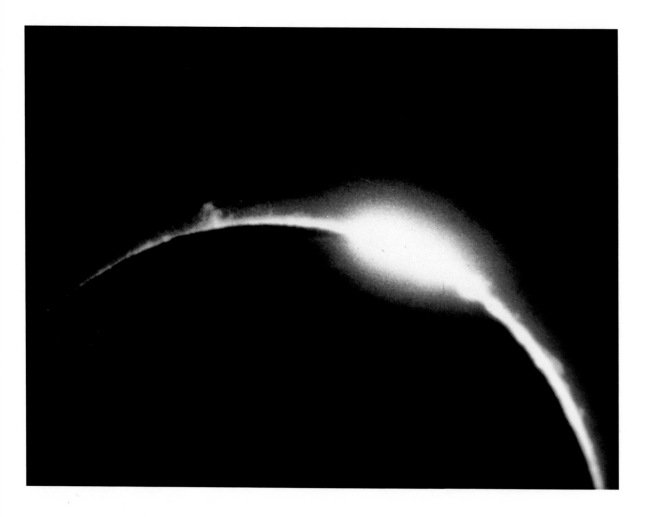

Radiation from the sun, seen here during a solar eclipse, can change the density of Earth's atmosphere and this, too, has an effect on the light coming from stars.

discoveries could be made with a telescope like this, it may seem surprising that scientists have not built and launched one so far. A telescope in space, however, would need a lot of attention by engineers and technicians. It would be very expensive to build, and a very large rocket would be required to launch it.

The United States does intend to put a telescope in space. It is the *Hubble Space Telescope*, or *HST*, and will be sent up in the shuttle during 1990. The HST is called an

optical telescope, because it will observe the universe using light, just as telescopes on Earth do.

There are, however, other ways of looking at objects in the universe. Apart from light, most objects send out energy in different forms, such as radio waves, x-rays, or very harmful nuclear radiation. *Electromagnetic radiation* includes visible light and various types of radiation. The spread of different forms of energy is called a spectrum. At one end of the spectrum are the radio waves that we use to receive radio and TV broadcasts. In the middle is visible light, flanked at one end by *infra-red* and at the other by *ultra-violet*. Both forms can be very harmful, just as radio waves can if the power is above a certain level. At the other end of the electromagnetic spectrum are harmful rays such as x-rays and *gamma rays*.

Astronomers use all forms of energy on the electromagnetic spectrum to learn certain details about the object that sent out the

What scientists call the electromagnetic spectrum goes from IR (infra-red) through visible light to UV (ultra-violet), far UV, x-rays, and gamma rays. Only some IR and all visible light reaches the surface of the Earth. To see objects in different portions of the spectrum it is necessary to go high up in the atmosphere or, in the case of some rays, far out into space to capture light in that part of the spectrum.

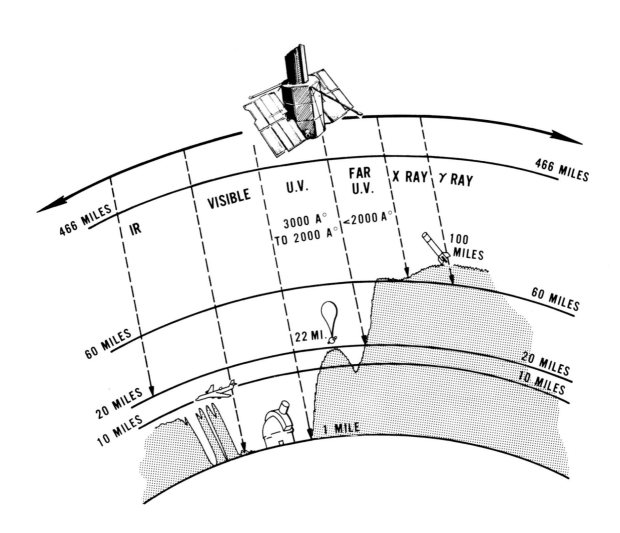

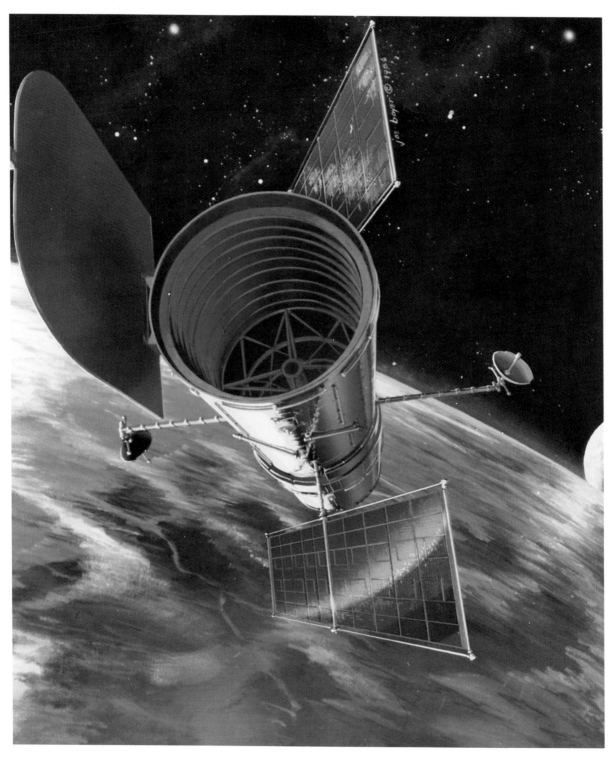

With this telescope, scientists will explore distant reaches of the universe hitherto unseen by any human eye.

The United States has organized an international team of astronomers to use the Hubble Space Telescope, which will enable scientists to see 350 times the volume of space visible to Earth-based astronomers.

energy. Light itself can tell a lot about the object from which it was sent. All matter is made up of *atoms*, and the light from that material contains lines that are seen when the light is passed through a prism. A prism is a triangular block of glass with flat sides. The arrangement of black lines is determined by the substance that is radiating the light.

Scientists study radio waves sent out by some objects in the universe to learn more about the object. X-rays and gamma rays can also give information about activity occurring in the object that radiated them. Examined together, light waves, radio waves, and hard radiation like x-rays and gamma rays help form a picture of the object — what it is made from, how long it has been producing energy, how big it is, and even, perhaps, why it acts the way it does and how long it will continue.

**The huge telescope is as big as some of the largest Earth-based observatories.**

# Solar Observatories

The nearest star to the Earth is the sun. It is a *thermonuclear reactor*, continuously "burning" like a nuclear bomb and releasing enormous amounts of matter and energy as a result. All matter is made up of atoms, and all atoms consist of a *nucleus* of *protons* and *neutrons* surrounded by orbiting *electrons*. More than 100 elements make up the contents of the universe, and the atoms in each element have a different number of protons and neutrons. Hydrogen, the lightest element, has just one proton and one neutron.

The sun releases energy because the temperature and pressure at its center are so great that hydrogen atoms literally fuse together and become helium, the second lightest element. This is also the process that occurs when hydrogen bombs explode. The sun loses more than 4 million tons of energy this way each second, but it is so big that the loss is barely noticeable. It has been doing this for about 4,500 million years and will continue to do so for at least another 5,000 million years.

From its vantage point in orbit, the manned Skylab space station launched in 1973 was used by three separate teams of astronauts to study the sun through the Apollo Telescope Mount, seen here as a white structure on top of the station.

The sun is vital to life on Earth. The planets were formed at the same time as the sun, and the sun provides the energy by which life thrives and develops. Because so many of our activities depend upon the sun, it is important that we understand it. Without the sun we would all die, and life would cease to exist on this planet or any other in the solar system.

*NASA*, the National Aeronautics and Space Administration, was formed in 1958 to develop America's non-military space activities.

**The Skylab Apollo Telescope Mount had its own solar cells, four wings that provided electrical power from sunlight.**

Scientists were particularly eager to use satellites to get up above the atmosphere and observe the sun over long periods. Solar observatories were an early choice for scientists who wanted to know more about how events on

19

the surface of our nearest star affected radio communication, weather, and changes in our climate.

The sun is a giant ball of gas, and the temperature at its surface is only a few thousand degrees. At the core, where nuclear reactions are continually taking place, the temperature is 14 million degrees. The surface has a wide range of spots and blemishes that come and go with time. Scientists want to know more about these. Sunspots appear black because they are cooler than the surrounding material, and they seem to be linked to particularly violent activity just below the surface.

To study all these strange events, NASA launched a series of *Orbiting Solar Observatory (OSO)* spacecraft beginning in 1962. From its orbiting position 350 miles above Earth, OSO observed the sun. In the first three months, OSO gathered three times as much information about the sun's x-ray emissions as had ever been gathered before. In all, NASA launched eight

**For almost a year scientists on Earth and astronauts in space were able to watch the sun through a complex array of scientific instruments and telescopes.**

**The study of the sun is important for a better understanding of the Earth's atmosphere, since radiation from our nearest star directly affects the behavior of our atmosphere.**

OSO spacecraft between 1962 and 1975 and in that time made many changes and modifications to the spacecraft design.

The OSO mission was to observe the sun in x-ray, ultraviolet, and infra-red portions of the spectrum. Only one spacecraft failed to make it into *orbit*, and the program was a great success. Some spacecraft also studied gamma rays coming in from outside the solar system, and one was fitted with equipment to measure x-rays from other stars.

Observations of ultraviolet radiation from the sun can reveal facts about what is going on inside the sun. Ultraviolet radiation does not reach the surface of the Earth in any great quantity, and those who wish to see activity in that part of the spectrum must do so from space. Much of what OSO saw and told scientists helped prepare the way for the next major step in solar studies, the launch of manned telescopes.

In 1973 NASA launched the giant orbiting space station called Skylab. One of the main purposes of this enormous workshop in space was to carry solar telescopes and have astronauts record events taking place on the surface of the sun. Skylab itself weighed almost 100 tons, and the huge assembly of telescopes weighed more than 12 tons.

The canister containing the telescopes was almost 15 feet long and 20 feet across. It had four enormous solar panels capable of supplying electrical power to all the experiments, the panels were 102 feet across. When fully extended from the folded position they were in at launch, the telescopes carried film canisters, and a special console inside the space station allowed an astronaut to point the

**Astronaut Owen Garriott controls the battery of solar telescopes aboard Skylab through a control panel on board.**

Astronaut Jack Lousma goes outside Skylab to change the canisters of film in the telescope's scientific instruments package.

telescopes at specific places on the sun and to operate the instruments.

The Skylab solar telescope was in almost continuous operation during all three manned missions to the space stations. These ended with the return to Earth of the last crew in early 1974. In that time the astronauts shot more than 150,000 pictures of the sun and gathered detailed information about many fascinating events taking place on this important star. Unfortunately, the launch of Skylab took place during a period of relatively quiet activity on the sun, and astronomers were unable to observe the more violent events that take place on a regular cycle.

For a long time it has been known that the sun goes through cycles of quiet and active events that occur on an 11-year cycle. NASA built a special spacecraft called the *Solar Maximum*

**To learn even more about the sun, NASA launched the Solar Maximum Mission satellite in 1980, carrying a battery of research instruments and telescopes which could send its information down to Earth by radio signal.**

*Mission (SMM)* to catch the sun during an active period. In this way, it was hoped, the spacecraft would be in space during the peak of the 11-year sunspot cycle and observe the number of sunspots in total. An important part of the mission was to measure precisely the total energy output of the sun over that 11-year period.

The SMM spacecraft was successfully launched by NASA in 1980. It was not as big as the Skylab telescopes, but Skylab had helped scientists choose just the right sort of instruments to concentrate on particular areas of research. The spacecraft was about 13 feet

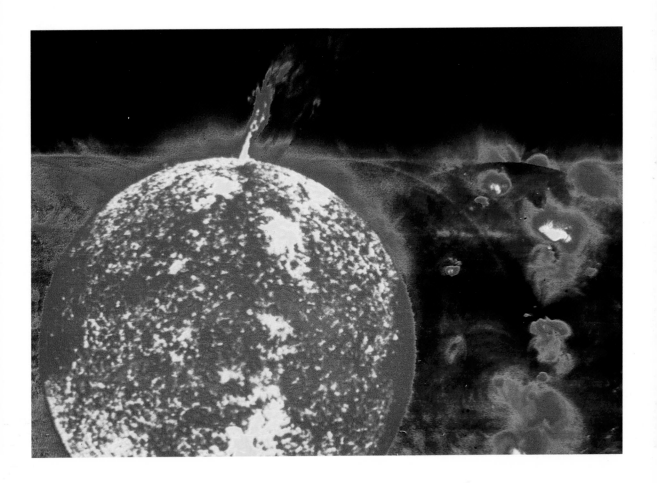

Seen through Skylab's solar telescopes, this massive burst of solar energy called a "prominence" is more than 200,000 miles long — approximately the distance between the Earth and the moon.

long, 7 feet in diameter, and weighed just over 2.5 tons. After eight months of operation, a problem developed with the spacecraft *attitude control*. It was put into a very slow roll to prevent it tumbling out of control.

Four of the experiments on board were useless, because in order to work they had to be precisely pointed at the sun. This was impossible with the spacecraft spinning. Then

This view, taken by the Solar Maximum Mission spacecraft in Earth orbit, shows the sun at the bottom left with radiation from the dense part of its inner atmosphere, called the "corona".

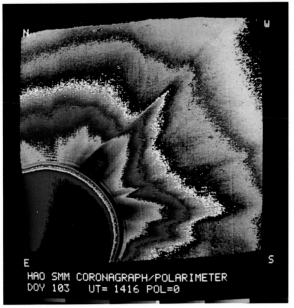

HAO SMM CORONAGRAPH/POLARIMETER
DOY 103    UT= 1416 POL=0

trouble developed with three instruments, and it looked as though the entire mission, including the $80 million spacecraft, would be lost. In 1984, however, a shuttle was able to rendezvous with the SMM, and astronauts repaired the attitude control equipment and fixed a couple of instruments aboard the spacecraft. It was restored to normal duty and is still working today.

Observing the sun will become easier when NASA launches a permanently manned space station in the late 1990s. The space station will not be like Skylab, which could be manned for only three periods during 1973 and 1974. The permanent space station will operate continuously for 20 or 30 years, and instruments will be attached to girders and beams designed to support many different activities.

**In 1984 shuttle astronauts visited the Solar Maximum Mission spacecraft to make minor repairs and change some of the instruments before putting it back into orbit.**

# Orbiting Observatories

Beyond the sun lies a *galaxy* of fascinating objects that Earth-based telescopes have discovered and investigated. The sun is a star, but is on our doorstep compared to the stars beyond. Astronomers believe that most stars have planets. They believe planets form as a result of the birth of a star, and that many planets around distant stars could support life. This possibility compels them to learn as much as they can about our universe.

Stars are grouped into galaxies, and each galaxy contains an average of 100,000 stars the size of our sun. Our sun is an average star, but some are very hot and others are cool. Scientists want to study stars as they are forming. Stars usually form in clusters deep inside dense pockets of gas and dust. When their nuclear

The Orbiting Astronomical Observatory, or OAO, satellite weighed more than two tons and carried experiments from many scientists interested in studying radiation from distant sources in the universe.

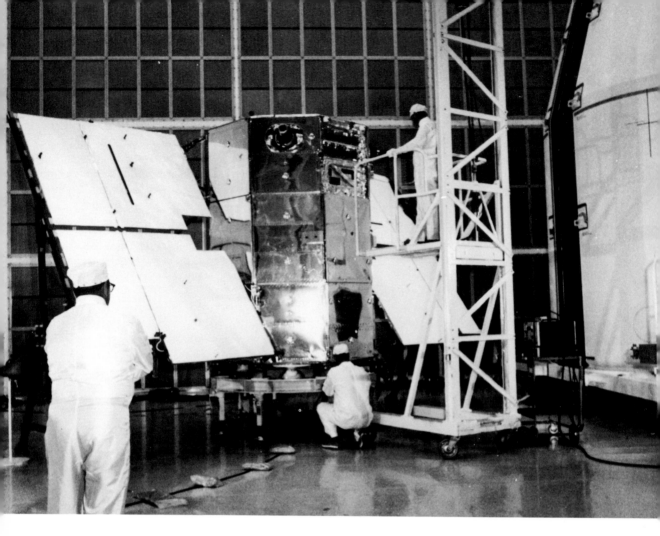

reactions start, they burst out with energy that helps blow the gas and dust away. Scientists want to study them just before they form and just afterward to compare the results.

At the other end of their life, stars do one of several things when they die, depending on their size. Comparatively small stars go out when the nuclear reactions stop. This happens when a certain percentage of hydrogen is converted to helium. The nuclear fusion process is snuffed out like dense smoke choking a fire, and the star no longer shines. It then collapses down into a dense ball and becomes what scientists call a *black dwarf*.

If the star is a little bigger than our sun, it has a different end. It has so much material inside that as nuclear reactions take over more and more of the core, the outer layers of the star puff up like a balloon inflating. Suddenly, the outer layers explode with violent energy. Enormous amounts

**Not all radiation from space that scientists are interested in observing reaches down to the surface of the Earth, so satellites like OAO are a vital part of fully understanding the nature of space.**

of material are flung off in all directions, and the star has literally blown itself apart. The core of the star collapses under the force of gravity into such a tight ball of matter that protons and neutrons are literally squeezed together.

Atomic particles do strange things when they are forced into so small a space. The protons become neutrons, and the star is said to be a *neutron star*. It still radiates energy left over from the final collapse, and it sends out a radio beam like a serachlight into space, Because it seems to pulse on and off as the rapidly spinning star flashes its beacon around the universe, the object is also called a *pulsar*.

28

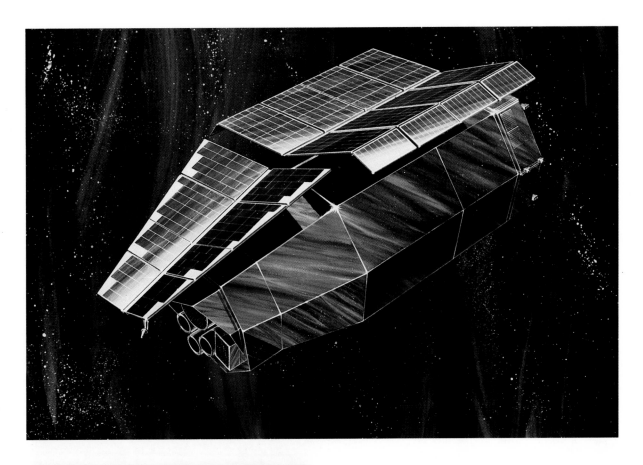

The first NASA High Energy Astronomy Observatory (HEAO 1) was launched in 1977 to study x-rays from many objects in the universe.

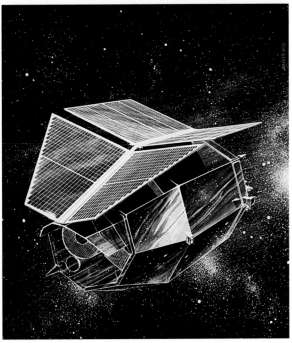

The beautiful Crab Nebula is a neutron star with a pulsar at its core. This exploded 4,400 years ago, but light traveling at 186,000 miles per second took more than 3,300 years to reach Earth. It suddenly appeared in the sky in the year 1054. People watching the sky were frightened and thought it was an evil sign. Yet the fate of becoming a neutron star is not the worst fate in the universe.

Very big stars end their days by going through

The second High Energy Astronomy Observatory satellite was equipped with instruments observing both x-ray and gamma-ray events in space.

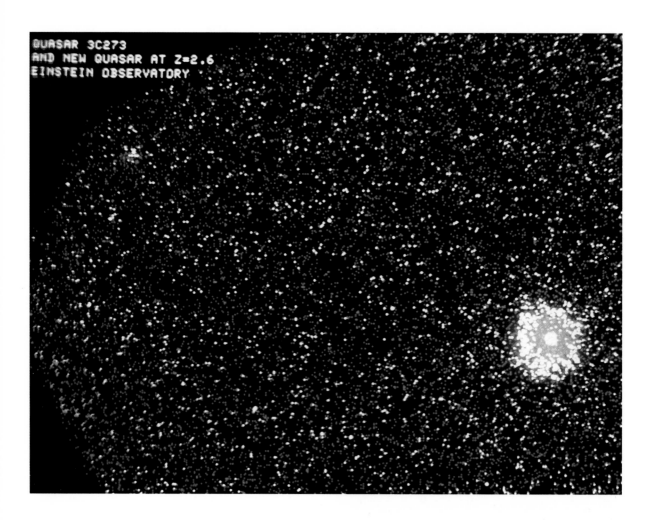

QUASAR 3C273
AND NEW QUASAR AT Z=2.6
EINSTEIN OBSERVATORY

**The brightest object in this picture, taken by a High Energy Astronomy Observatory satellite, was believed to be more than ten billion light years from Earth.**

a stage similar to that of a neutron star. Instead of compressing down until the very particles of which the star's atoms are made are touching, all the matter that made up the star collapses totally into a *black hole.* A black hole is so small it theoretically cannot exist. Mathematicians say such a thing cannot be.

Astronomers say they have evidence that black holes exist. They believe that black holes bend space and time and do other things we cannot imagine. Together, mathematicians and scientists agree that there is only one way a black hole can be real. Both say that if the black hole bends space and time, it could be a funnel through which the matter that made up the dead star is channeled to another part of the universe and another time, either in the past or in the future.

This sounds extraordinary, yet it is the only way the theory can be turned into reality. Nothing else works, and every other idea about black holes runs into a dead end. Is there somewhere in the universe that vast quantities of matter are being produced seemingly out of nowhere? Yes. They are called *quasars.* Astronomers first detected quasars many years ago and now believe them to be the funnels through which old galaxies formed. If they are the places where dead stars throw up old matter, it is the perfect re-cycling device.

The third and last High Energy Astronomy Observatory satellite is prepared at Cape Canaveral, Florida, for its launch in 1979.

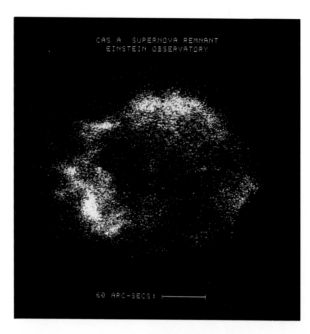

CAS A SUPERNOVA REMNANT
EINSTEIN OBSERVATORY

60 ARC-SECS:

Totally invisible to the naked eye, this strange x-ray picture shows a massive star explosion which is believed to have taken place in the year 1657.

To study pulsars, black holes, and quasars, scientists built a series of spacecraft called *Orbiting Astronomical Observatories (OAO)*. Four OAO spacecraft were built and launched between 1966 and 1972, but only two worked. Nevertheless, the information they sent back to Earth helped confirm the existence of black holes. NASA wanted a more powerful set of instruments and built the *High Energy Astronomy Observatory (HEAO)* satellites.

X-rays, gamma rays, and cosmic radiation from deep parts of the galaxy record the activity associated with pulsars, black holes, and quasars. The three HEAO satellites were built to

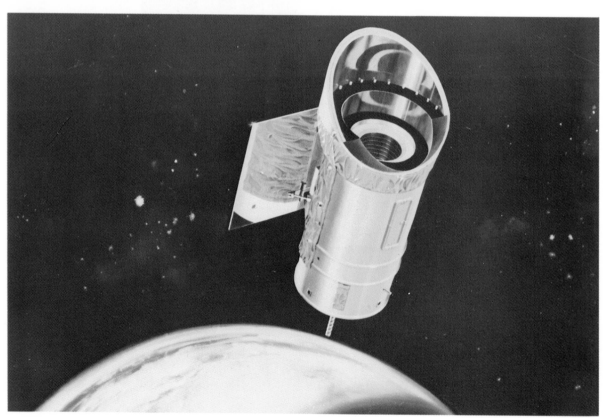

IRAS was designed to study infra-red radiation from stars and galaxies in the universe.

Technicians prepare the Infra-Red Astronomy Satellite (IRAS) for launch in 1983.

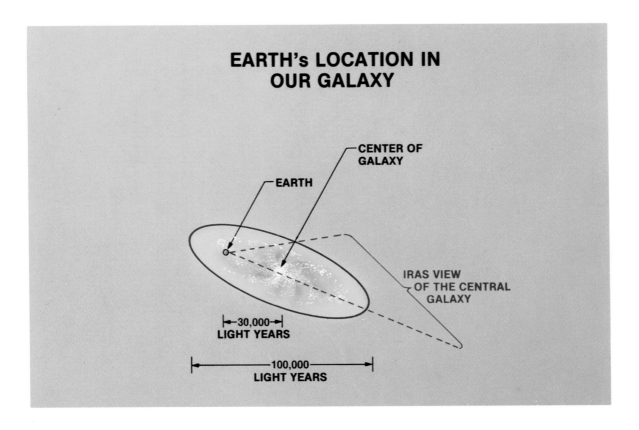

## EARTH's LOCATION IN OUR GALAXY

CENTER OF GALAXY

EARTH

IRAS VIEW OF THE CENTRAL GALAXY

|←—30,000—→|
LIGHT YEARS

←————————100,000————————→
LIGHT YEARS

tackle these issues head on. They were very complex spacecraft and provided scientists with large amounts of information about these strange objects. *HEAO 1* and *HEAO 3* were built as scanning telescopes designed to study the wide range of events going on all across the sky. *HEAO 2* was built to study specific events and objects.

*HEAO 1* was designed for six months of useful observation and continued to work for seventeen months before it failed. *HEAO 2* was sent up in 1978 packed with highly advanced scientific instruments for detailed study of x-ray sources. X-rays are one of the tell-tale signs of a black hole. Black holes are totally invisible, and they swallow light from objects that fall into them. For instance, if a star fell into a black hole, it would collapse into the hole at the speed of light. Light from the star radiating out would be swallowed down also, and nothing could be seen.

Because they cannot be seen, the only way to know a black hole exists is to watch what happens to dust and gas that gets too close. It is

From our location in space, IRAS gets a clear view across the center of our galaxy, where many densely packed infra-red sources of radiation can be found.

sucked down the black hole, and just at the very edge, before it plunges down forever, it heats up and gives off x-rays. What HEAO found was positive proof that black holes exist by measuring some suspicious objects in the galaxy. It was further proof that the black hole is real, and that quasars really might be the other end of a funnel.

In 1983, another observatory was launched to examine strange objects in the universe. Called the *Infra-Red Astronomical Satellite,* or *IRAS,* it was a cooperative project between the United States, Britain, and the Netherlands. It operated for ten months, making the first full sky survey of infra-red sources in the universe. Before IRAS, only 1,000 infra-red objects in the sky had been located. The satellite found another 250,000.

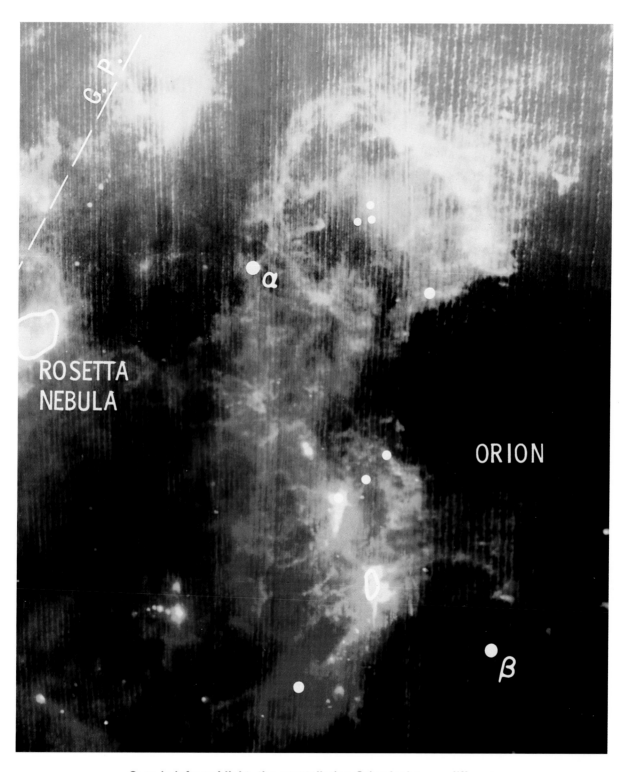

Seen in infra-red light, the constellation Orion looks very different.

# Hubble Space Telescope

The biggest advance in optical astronomy since the invention of the telescope in the seventeenth century will be achieved when a NASA shuttle launches the Hubble Space Telescope into space sometime in 1990. With this instrument, an international team of astronomers will observe objects in the universe 50 times dimmer than the faintest object currently seen by Earth-based telescopes. It will be able to see planets around the stars nearest to us, and it will probably be able to look back in time to the origin of the universe.

Scientists believe the universe began about 12 billion years ago. Light travels at 186,000 miles per second. On Earth, we see things virtually as they happen because light travels so fast. As distances become greater, however, even that enormous speed takes measurable time to reach us. Shine a flashlight from the moon and its light would take more than one second to reach us. The light from the sun takes six hours to reach Earth. Light from the nearest star takes more than three years. We say it is just over three light years away from our solar system.

The galaxy is 100 billion light years across, and therefore light from a star on one side takes 100 billion years to reach the other side. The galaxy to which we belong is called the Milky Way. Galaxies are several million light years apart. Because astronomers believe the universe began at a particular point in space around 12 billion years ago, if we could see objects 12 billion light years away, we would see the beginning of time. From Earth we are limited to objects about half this distance away.

The Hubble Space Telescope will see a distance of 12 billion light years and more, taking in a part of the universe 350 times

The Hubble Space Telescope is shown in the Lockheed test chamber, where it will be exposed to conditions it is expected to operate in when it reaches orbit.

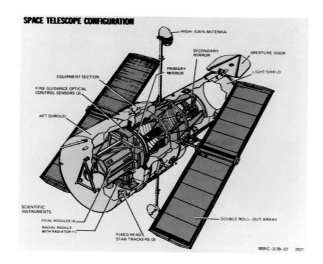

SPACE TELESCOPE CONFIGURATION

The Space Telescope is a complex observatory, equipped with computers and transmission equipment for sending its information down to Earth.

larger than has ever been seen before. This is because the telescope can see objects not only 50 times fainter, but also 7 times farther away. Today, astronomers know of at least 100 billion stars in our own galaxy and of at least 100 billion galaxies. The Hubble Telescope will open up a window back in time to the earliest days of the universe.

The Space Telescope must be protected by special aluminum foil from the intense changes of temperature it will experience between the night and day sides of the Earth as it orbits the planet.

One of two solar panels that the Space Telescope will unfold to convert sunlight into electricity is seen here, attached firmly to the side of the forward section.

Technicians in Lockheed's specially prepared checkout room hook up the Space Telescope to monitor its electrical systems.

NASA began planning for the telescope during the 1970s, and in 1977 Congress finally gave its approval to build the huge spacecraft. At launch it will weigh almost 13 tons and consist of a tube 43 feet, 6 inches in length with a diameter of 14 feet. Two large side panels will be unfurled in space. Each will measure almost 8 feet wide by more than 39 feet long and contain thousands of solar cells for converting sunlight into electricity.

The telescope will not be manned by an observer. Instead, special modules will contain equipment designed to record images on film or send information down to Earth on a radio signal. The heart of the spacecraft is the cassegrain telescope with its 94.5-inch primary mirror. Images reflected by that mirror bounce back 16 feet up to the secondary mirror, which is 12 inches in diameter. This mirror narrows and intensifies the beam of light and reflects it back again to the main mirror and through a 24-inch hole in the middle to the instruments at the back.

The primary mirror alone weighs almost a ton, and special precautions have been taken to see that it does not distort in the vacuum of

The upper part of the Space Telescope is about to be lowered onto the aft section which carries the main mirror.

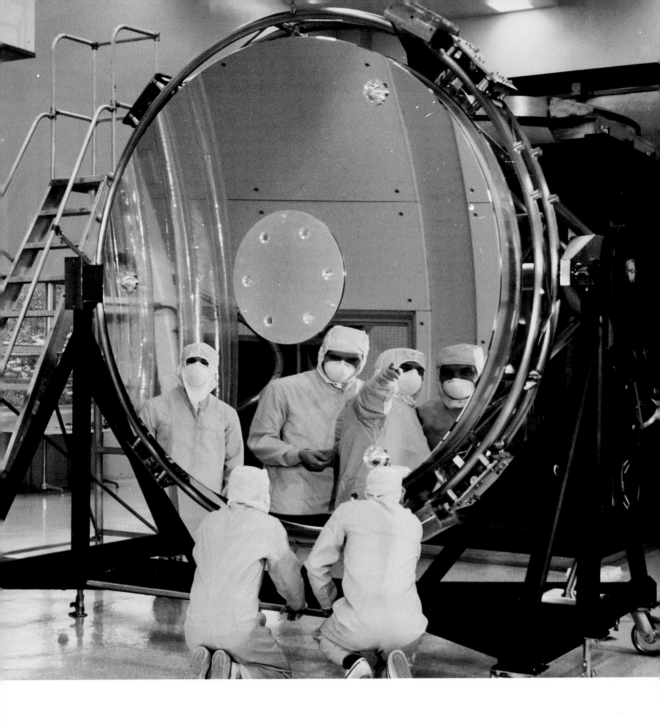

space. At the back of the telescope special modules carry instruments that can be changed from time to time. Scientists working with the telescope on Earth will prepare special instruments for astronauts to carry into space. From time to time the shuttle will rendezvous with the telescope and astronauts will perform a space walk to change the modules.

**The main Space Telescope mirror is 94 inches in diameter and technicians must wear masks and special suits to maintain absolute cleanliness at the mirror's surface.**

The pointing accuracy of the telescope achieves levels never before attained in a space-based observatory. It will have special electronically controlled gyroscopes to keep it pointing very precisely at the object being viewed. Its accuracy can be compared to standing in Washington, D.C., and viewing a dime located in Boston. If the telescope could extend a beam 600 miles long, it would be sufficiently stable that the far end of the beam would move no more than 1.2 inches off center.

Five main instruments have been selected for the first mission of the Hubble Space Telescope. Four are from the United States and one is European. The first experiment is a special camera that can take wide shots of large areas containing objects such as galaxies and quasars. It will sharpen up the view of blurred, distant objects like these. Alternatively, it can be used to take good quality pictures of the planets.

At the distance of Jupiter, it will show detail equal to that taken by the two Voyager flyby spacecraft that shot the best pictures so far of Jupiter. It will do so as often as necessary on a regular basis. This will enable astronomers to build up a time-lapse picture of changes on the

**With an accuracy never before achieved for an astronomical observatory on Earth or in space, technicians check the precise shape and size of the main mirror.**

Technicians attach wiring and harnesses from the folded solar panels to the main structure of the Space Telescope.

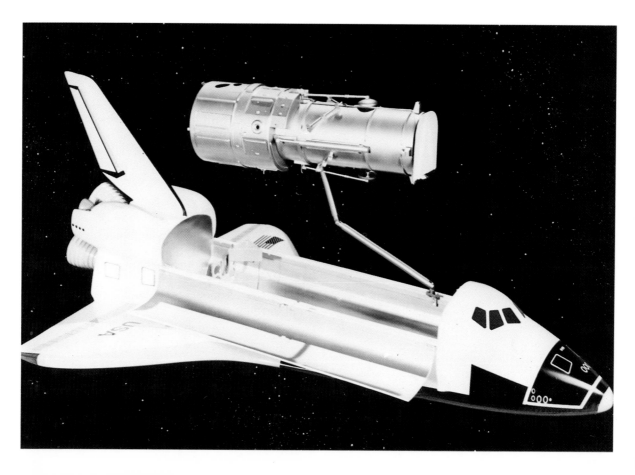

**The Space Telescope is carried into orbit aboard the NASA shuttle and gently off-loaded using the special arm on the orbiter.**

giant outer planets like Jupiter and Saturn.

Another instrument will study very faint objects at great distance. It will view them in ultraviolet and visible light and project the light through a prism to study the material of which the object is made. This helps identify what the object is, what it is composed of, and how it might be expected to behave in future. It will study the insides of galaxies and mysterious jets of matter that spurt from quasars.

The third instrument will call upon the full

**Shown here folded into a tube-like assembly, one of two solar panels provided by the European Space Agency is being checked out prior to installation aboard the Space Telescope.**

power of the telescope to get detailed views of dim objects. It will view these objects in small scale, looking to measure them in specific areas without concern about looking at the complete object. It will be set up to look at the object in ultraviolet light, which scientists believe is the best for understanding the composition of objects in the universe.

The fourth instrument is the simplest of all. It uses the precise pointing stability of the telescope to measure the light from a single object. It will do this with great accuracy and will be particularly useful for observing fast-spinning stars like neutron stars and pulsars. It will be able to detect minor changes in the amount of light coming from different sides of a spinning star at the end of its life.

The last instrument is provided by the European Space Agency. It will collect and concentrate very faint light from feeble stars and help provide scientists with information about large clusters of stars, big but cool stars, planets around nearby stars, and huge clouds of gas in galaxies. By studying the center of galaxies with this instrument, it may be possible to find new black holes. Using telescopes on Earth, astronomers believe they have found traces of such strange objects already. The Space Telescope will help find out if they are right.

More than 380 years ago, Galileo turned a telescope on the heavens and started a

**Once in orbit, the Space Telescope's solar panels are unfolded and it begins to receive electrical energy from the sun.**

revolution in astronomy. NASA will extend that revolution further with the introduction of the Space Telescope. A special institute has been set up to manage all the results that will come from this spacecraft. Scientists from all over the world will gather to decide what new experiments to provide and to coordinate the scientific study of the heavens. Records of this information will be preserved at the institute, and members of the public will be given summaries of the results.

Some people question why the U.S. is spending money on the Hubble Space

Using technology developed for the Space Telescope, NASA would like to develop this observatory for looking at x-ray sources in the universe.

Telescope. According to astronomers, there are many reasons. Perhaps the best reason is that as humans we can never understand ourselves fully unless we first understand our surroundings. On clear nights, our universe is laid out before us. The Hubble Telescope may lead to answers about how the universe began and how it has changed with time.

# GLOSSARY

| | |
|---|---|
| Atom | The smallest quantity of an element that can take part in a chemical reaction. Atoms take the form of a small nucleus of particles surrounded by one or more electrons. |
| Attitude control | The small motors that balance a satellite and keep it in exactly the right spot. |
| Black dwarf | A dense ball of matter; the left-over remains of a collapsed star that has ceased to produce nuclear energy. |
| Black hole | A collapsed star of great mass; no longer producing nuclear reactions to keep it inflated, the star has crashed down into an infinite point. |
| Electromagnetic radiation | Radiation consisting of combined electrical and magnetic forces. |
| Electron | A stable particle found in all atoms orbiting the nucleus of protons and electrons and carrying a negative electrical charge. |
| Galaxy | A large accumulation of stars, numbering several hundred million in each cluster, usually gathered together in the form of a rotating spiral. |
| Gamma rays | Electro-magnetic radiation with very short wavelengths. |
| Gravity | The force of attraction that moves or tends to move bodies toward the center of a celestial body such as the Earth or moon. |
| High Energy Astronomy Observatory (HEAO) | A series of four satellites built to investigate the universe with powerful telescopes in the non-visible portion of the spectrum. |
| Hubble Space Telescope (HST) | A telescope NASA plans to launch during early 1990 that will have the ability to see 350 times the volume of space presently visible to Earth-based astronomers. |
| Infra-red | The part of the electromagnetic spectrum with a longer wavelength than light but a shorter wavelength than radio waves. Like radio waves, infra-red radiation cannot be seen with the unaided human eye. |
| Infra-Red Astronomical Satellite (IRAS) | A cooperative satellite project between the United States, Britain, and the Netherlands, launched in 1983 to map the universe in infra-red light. |
| NASA | National Aeronautics and Space Administration, set up in October 1958 for the peaceful exploration of space. |
| Neutrons | A particle without any electrical charge found in the nucleus of an atom. |
| Neutron star | A massive star that collapses down until nothing is left except a ball of neutrons at the core. |
| Nucleus | The core of an atom, usually containing varying numbers of protons and neutrons. |

| | |
|---|---|
| Orbit | The curved path, usually almost circular, followed by a planet or satellite in its motion around another planet in space. |
| Orbiting Solar Observatory (OSO) | A series of spacecraft launched between 1962 and 1975, built to observe the sun from Earth orbit. |
| Orbiting Astronomical Observatories (OAO) | Four spacecraft built and launched between 1966 and 1972, designed to observe the universe and help confirm the existence of black holes. |
| Proton | A stable nuclear particle with a positive electrical charge, found in the nucleus of an atom. The number of protons determines the element (material) formed by all the particles. |
| Pulsar | A star that appears to blink on and off as it sends out a beam of radio energy in a single direction like a search light, flashing as it rotates past an observer. |
| Quasars | First detected in 1963, powerful sources of radio waves and other forms of energy. |
| Reflector | A type of telescope in which the initial image is formed on a mirror and reflected to a magnifying lens. |
| Refractor | A telescope designed to magnify an object by passing the light from it through a series of lenses to an eyepiece. |
| Solar Maximum Mission (SMM) | A spacecraft launched by NASA in 1980 with a battery of powerful telescopes to observe the sun for long periods. |
| Thermonuclear reactor | A place where great temperatures and high pressures create violent motion between atoms causing the particles in the atomic nucleus to fuse together and thereby liberate enormous quantities of energy. |
| Ultraviolet light | The part of the electromagnetic spectrum with wavelengths shorter than light, invisible to the naked eye. |
| X-rays | Electromagnetic radiation between ultra-violet and gamma radiation on the electromagnetic spectrum. Electromagnetic radiation with higher energy than x-rays commonly originates in the violent nuclear reactions of stars. |

# INDEX

Page numbers in *italics* refer to photographs or illustrations.

## DATE DUE

| JAN 1 4 | | | |
|---|---|---|---|
| FEB 2 5 | | | |
| 1/10/02 | | | |
| | | | |
| | | | |
| | | | |
| | | | |
| | | | |
| | | | |
| | | | |
| | | | |
| | | | |
| | | | |
| | | | |
| | | | |
| | | | |

DEMCO 38-297